THE TIBETAN BUDDHIST
HOME ALTAR

THE TIBETAN BUDDHIST HOME ALTAR

Practical and Spiritual Advice

Buddhist Practices for Daily Life Using
Your Personal Altar

By
Geshe Dakpa Topgyal

 library partners press
a digital publishing imprint

Produced and Distributed By:

Library Partners Press
ZSR Library
Wake Forest University
1834 Wake Forest Road
Winston-Salem, North Carolina 27106

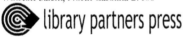 library partners press

a digital publishing imprint

www.librarypartnerspress.org

Manufactured in the United States of America

This book is
dedicated
to all its readers.

May this book
benefit
their spiritual growth and well-being.

May this book also
help
all readers to see meaning in the
merit-making practice of offering material objects
to the
Enlightened Beings.

ACKNOWLEDGEMENTS

I must not forget to express thanks to my devoted students,

Ms. Pamela Harrod,
Ms. Sara Graham,
Dr. Cheryl Novak Condy,
Ms. Grace Rice, and
Ms. Kristin Hess

for their tireless efforts in transcribing, editing, proof reading, and finally putting together this book in a very concise and easy-to-read manner, so that all levels of interested readers can benefit from it.

I acknowledge that this book would not be among one of the Dharma books you read without the above Dharma students' generous work.

HOMAGE

Merit is an indispensable condition for spiritual
growth.
To all Buddhas, Bodhisattvas, and root gurus,
Who are the ultimate sources of the merit field,
I respectfully prostrate and pay homage through
body, speech, and mind by
kneeling down on the bare ground.

CONTENTS

INTRODUCTION

Everywhere you go to Buddhist temples and private Buddhist family shrine rooms, you may see a decorative altar displayed with various sacred images, holy texts, and material offerings as well as money. Many people get the impression that Buddhists worship idols and waste fresh material things like fresh fruits, fresh flowers, etc., and that these offerings serve no good purpose. Some open-minded and sincerely interested people in Buddhism often wonder: What is the significance of material offerings, and what is the purpose of displaying sacred images and holy texts in the best room of the house, keeping it exceptionally neat and clean in a respectful way? There must be a valid reason and spiritual significance behind it.

The main reason why I chose to write a short book on the Tibetan Buddhist altar and the significance behind it is to help people interested in Buddhism to understand the purpose and meaning of the Buddhist altar. This book will also help people set up a traditional Buddhist altar in their own home or in any place conducive to doing their daily Dharma practice.

In general, doing Dharma practice at the place where there are spiritually inspiring sacred images of Enlightened Beings, holy texts, and symbolic material offerings of fresh flowers, fruits, illuminating light, and fragrant incense, etc., helps you to have a feeling of devotion, trust, respect, humility, and admiration towards enlightened qualities of Buddhas and Bodhisattvas. These feelings must be the active qualities of mind that are ready to embark on Dharma practice. Therefore, the actual purpose of the altar is an external aid to generate these positive qualities of mind in order for your Dharma practice to become effective and powerful.

The purpose of displaying sacred images and holy texts is to remind one of the kindness of Buddha and to reaffirm your commitment to follow the path laid out by the compassionate teacher Shakyamuni Buddha. Similarly, the purpose of arranging attractive material offerings before the images of Enlightened Beings is a token of appreciation and expression of one's devotion, respect, and humility. It is surely not an act of worshipping an idol.

The true feeling of devotion, respect, humility, and loyalty in your spiritual path are the most indispensable positive aspects of your mind. It is important to make an effort to acquire these qualities in your heart and mind.

I hope that this small book on the Tibetan Buddhist altar is useful for every reader to understand the real spiritual meaning of the altar and its significance to the actual Dharma practice of internalizing the path within you.

With prayers,
Geshe Dakpa Topgyal

SECTION ONE

THE TIBETAN BUDDHIST HOME ALTAR

Part One

THE TIBETAN BUDDHIST ALTAR

An altar (Cho-sham) is a special place for the display of sacred images. Any person who would like to arrange an altar in their home may do so; however, they should first have a proper understanding of arrangement, procedures, and significance. This book will provide a detailed discussion of the elements of a traditional altar as well as explanations of the activities associated with making offerings. Most important of all are the explanations of the mental attitudes that will be most beneficial to the practitioner in terms of spiritual growth.

The dimensions of a traditional home altar are as follows: 30" H x 18"-24" W x 30"-36" L. This size allows room for four or five statues and enough extra room for other objects and for offerings. The height of the altar is at the eye level of a practitioner seated on a floor cushion, with no need for him or her to look upward or downward. The size of the altar may be modified to suit a particular room or any particular situation. If the condition of the surface of the altar table is good, there is no need for an altar cloth. If the condition is not good, or if you merely prefer, you may use an altar cloth made of brocade, cotton, or linen. Wool is not used, nor should a towel or bed sheet be used.

The four major parts of an altar display are:

1. A physical image of Buddha
2. Holy texts
3. Stupa (pagoda)
4. Various material offerings

1. The physical image of Buddha is known as a rupakaya, or the physical body of an Enlightened Being. It can be in the form of a statue or a thangkha, which is a painted or printed scroll or wall hanging depicting an Enlightened Being. Once you have acquired an image of Buddha, you should take it to a lama or a monk to have it blessed. The blessing activates the life force of the image. The rupakaya serves as a medium through which teachings are transmitted. The physical body of an Enlightened Being is purified, free of karmic obstructions, karmic lethargy, and unserviceability, which is a tendency for the body or the mind to become ill and dysfunctional with overuse.

The purpose of displaying a rupakaya is for it to act as an external aid to feelings of reverence and respect. Viewing an image of Buddha should make a practitioner feel calm and humble and serve as an antidote to arrogance, pride, and carelessness. The rupakaya is a spiritual reminder, not an object of worship.

2. The holy texts are considered the highest objects of reverence on the altar. They are symbols of the speech and teachings of an Enlightened Being. Highly developed practitioners can view them as the actual speech of

Buddha. An example of a text that may be on the altar is the Prajnaparamita Sutra.

3. A stupa is a symbol of the omniscient mind of an Enlightened Being, which is also known as the dharmakaya or truth body. The dharmakaya can directly and simultaneously perceive the ultimate truth of emptiness and the conventional truth of appearance as a non-dual single entity. The stupa must also be consecrated by a lama or monk to activate its spiritual force.

4. All material offerings must come from positive, clean, and wholesome sources. In his teachings on the Noble Eightfold Path to Enlightenment, Buddha included the Right Means of Livelihood. In addition to professions that involve killing, stealing, and lying, he included the following forbidden methods of obtaining life's necessities as well as altar offerings:

A) Flattery – the intention to acquire something by using complimentary words to influence others.
B) Hinting.
C) Seeking personal reward for a favor.
D) Through pretentious behavior – claiming power or influence that you do not actually have. Lying about spiritual attainments for personal benefit, such as claiming clairvoyance or psychic capabilities are very negative acts.
E) Contrived means – deception through setting up a contrived situation or prearranging circumstances to enhance personal benefit.

Engaging in making offerings before your meditation or sadhana practice is conducive to a successful practice because your mind becomes calm and filled with positive qualities. Lama Tsong-Khapa, the founder of the Gelugpa school of Tibetan Buddhism, gave another reason for making offerings to Enlightened Beings in his Lamrim Chenmo. He said, "The effective practice of making offerings before Enlightened Beings in a proper manner with respect and humility is an essential factor in increasing and enhancing the mental ability to understand and experience the Dharma more easily.

The practice is especially necessary for those who have serious problems with retaining what has been heard through listening to Dharma teachings, with being unable to comprehend the meaning of Dharma in spite of repeated contemplation, and being unable to successfully gain personal experience of Dharma no matter how much they meditate on a given aspect." These problems are due to the unserviceability of the mind caused by the presence of heavy karmic and delusive mental obstructions.

These problems can be helped and overcome by the serious effort of engaging in the practice of making offerings every day with the sole intention of increasing one's mental capacity.

Offerings placed on the altar usually fall into one of the following categories:

A. Clear water / Argam in Skt (Sanskrit)
B. Scented water for washing feet / Padham in Skt
C. Scented water for bathing / Gandha in Skt
D. Flowers / Puspa in Skt
E. Incense / Dupo in Skt
F. Light / Aloka or Dipa in Skt
G. Fruit or high quality cookies / Naivdya in Skt
H. Music / Shabta in Skt

The following instructions stress the wholesome source, freshness, and high quality of offerings as well as the correct way to prepare them with a humble, respectful, sincere, and deeply committed attitude. Recitations and prayers are suggested for each type of offering that serve to multiply the merit you acquire and also multiply the number and quality of the offerings in the eyes of Enlightened Beings.

Offerings of light, incense, water, and music may be made daily. Fruit and flower offerings may remain on the altar until they are no longer fresh. Money offerings are sometimes placed on altars in temples or Dharma centers and are solely used to purchase candles, incense, flowers, and other offerings. It is not appropriate to put family pictures on the altar.

Part Two

CLEAR WATER OFFERING

Clear Water. In Tibet, a clear water offering (Argam) could traditionally be obtained from the many mountain rivers and streams. In many areas of Tibet this is no longer possible. In the mid 1980's and early 1990's, China began the terribly destructive practice of dumping nuclear waste into Tibet's pristine river gorges. This contamination not only affects Tibet, but also India, Pakistan, Bangladesh, and China itself, because the major rivers of the East have their origins on the Tibetan plateau.

Classically, a clear water offering has eight great natural qualities: cooling, refreshing, tasty, clear, smooth sensation, free of bad odor, soothing to the throat, and harmless to the stomach. In modern times such perfect water is hard to find. You may use the best water that is available to your means and circumstances. Bottled water is acceptable. If tap water is used, the faucet should be clean, the temperature cool, and the pitcher used should be clean.

There is no fixed number of bowls, but Tibetan custom is to use seven water offering bowls. The number seven is considered auspicious and lucky. The material of the bowl is similar to the butter lamp bowl, with the addition of steel and wood. The bowls should be carefully washed and dried with a small clean towel made of cotton or wool felt.

The method of filling the bowls is to pour a small amount of water into the first bowl, then pour that water into the second bowl and place the first bowl on the altar. Pour the water from the second bowl into the third bowl and so on until all of the bowls are arranged on the altar in a line. This initial wetting of the bowls symbolizes that your mind is saturated with positive thoughts and intentions, such as love and compassion. The space between each bowl should be the distance of a grain of rice. Allowing the bowls to touch means that your ego is exerting itself to exaggerate its power. Leaving a large space between the bowls is inauspicious and means that you are too distant from the teachings and the teacher. An analogy to remember is that being too close to a fire will burn you and being too far away will give you no comfort.

After moistening the bowls, you should reaffirm your sense of mindfulness, humility, and respect. Fill the bowls starting from your left and moving to your right. Each bowl should be filled with a single continuous stream of water, beginning with a thin stream, then with a thicker stream, and ending with a thin stream. The slender streams at the beginning and end of filling each bowl symbolize sharp discernment wisdom. The larger mid-stream symbolizes courage, determination, and strong willpower in facing the difficulties of satisfying the multiple needs of sentient beings.

In the evening, the bowls should be washed and dried and placed upside down on a clean cloth or paper towel. The water from the offering bowls may be poured on plants outside or in the home. Never pour the water in a sink or toilet. It is suggested that water offerings be made at sunrise and disassembled at sunset.

During the first and last parts of filling each bowl, you may say to yourself:

May I attain sharp discernment wisdom like Shariputra.
(Shariputra was one of Buddha Shakyamuni's two main disciples.)

During the middle portion of filling each bowl, you may say to yourself:

May I attain courage and determination like Samantabhadra.
(Or, you may use the Bodhisattva Jampel. Both were known for
highly developed courage.)

Leave a small space the size of a grain of rice at the top of
each bowl. When all have been filled you may make one of
the following wishes or dedications:

May the act of offering water before Enlightened Beings help all
sentient beings to experience
and gain calm, peaceful, and supple minds that bring true inner
peace and joy.
May the act of offering water before Enlightened Beings help to
create merit that dispels karmic
dirt from the minds of all sentient beings.

One should recite the following mantra upon completion
of the clear water offering:

Om Sarva Tatha Gatha Sa Pari Vara Argam Pati Tsa Yeh
Soha
I send forth this clean and fresh water (with excellent
qualities of smell, taste, and freshness) to the assembly of
Enlightened Beings and Bodhisattvas with their retinue, the
ultimate source of refuge and the path to Enlightenment.

Part Three

SCENTED WATER OFFERING FOR BATHING OR WASHING FEET

Scented Water (Gandha). The water used and the method of filling the offering bowls are the same as described above. One or two drops of a natural scented plant extract should be used for each bowl, with rosewater, sandalwood extract, or saffron being traditional scents. You may divide the three types of water offerings among the bowls on your altar, with first priority given to fresh water for drinking, second priority to scented water for bathing, and third priority to scented water for washing feet. Hold in mind the values of each type as you make the offerings.

You may make the following dedication or wish:

May the act of offering scented water before the Enlightened Beings create merit to remove the negativities of moral corruption of all sentient beings.

Moral corruption destroys the strength and purity of our spiritual practice just as one drop of blood can spoil a pitcher of milk. This prayer can have a strong impact on your mind to develop love, compassion, and concern for the spiritual well being of all. Your mind will become calmer, neutral, and less influenced by bias and discrimination. This quality of mind is a precondition to successful practice.

One should recite the following mantra upon completion of the scented water offering:

Om Sarva Tatha Gatha Sa Pari Vara Gandha Pati Tsa Yeh Soha
I send forth this scented water to the assembly of Enlightened Beings and Bodhisattvas with their retinue, the ultimate source of refuge and the path to Enlightenment.

Scented water for Washing Feet (Padham). The practice of washing your own feet with scented cold water in the early morning and before going to bed helps to enhance the function of the nervous system by promoting optimal circulation of blood and energy and to aid our general physical health. The purpose of offering scented water for washing feet before Buddha is to create merit for all sentient beings to develop pure ethical conduct, which will enhance their healthy spiritual development.

One should recite the following mantra upon completion of the scented water for bathing offering:

Om Sarva Tatha Gatha Sa Pari Vara Padham Pati Tsa Yeh Soha

I send forth this scented water for bathing to the assembly of Enlightened Beings and Bodhisattvas with their retinue, the ultimate source of refuge and the path to Enlightenment.

Part Four

Fresh Flowers. The significance of offering flowers (Puspa) is that they are a reminder of impermanence. All things and phenomena are impermanent regardless of their beauty. Everything is subject to change, aging, death, and disintegration by its own nature, with no need to encounter any secondary external destructive force. Dharmakirti said, "All conditioned things are of impermanent and ever-changing nature because the mechanism of disintegration is built within their systems. The process of disintegration has begun from the first moment things come into being."

There are two types of impermanence. The first is the impermanence of the physical continuum, which is our ordinary understanding that nothing is going to last forever, with objects and phenomena more or less in a state of stasis, just waiting to meet with some external destructive force. The second and spiritually significant understanding of impermanence is the much more subtle one described by Dharmakirti; the impermanence of momentariness in which every object is in a constant state of change moving toward annihilation.

One should recite the following mantra upon completion of the fresh flowers offering:

Om Sarva Tatha Gatha Sa Pari Vara Puspa Pati Tsa Yeh Soha
I send forth this fresh, colorful, and fragrant flower to the
assembly of Enlightened Beings and Bodhisattvas with their retinue,
the ultimate source of refuge and the path to Enlightenment.

Part Five

FRAGRANT NATURAL INCENSE OFFERING

Incense. The source of an incense offering (Dupo) must be a natural material such as saffron, juniper, azalea leaf, pinewood or pinesap, eaglewood (agallock), or sandalwood. Sandalwood is a protected wood in India and only limbs that have fallen to the ground are supposed to be used. Other medicinal herbs are also often used. Musk, although very fragrant, is forbidden as it is an animal product. Trained and experienced people, often monks, collect and dry the substances under particular conditions and temperatures. The ingredients are then mixed in amounts that produce a mild, soothing, and relaxing scent.

The functions of burning incense are: (1) to purify contaminated air by destroying bad odors and impurities and (2) to relieve contaminated stagnant energy in our body in a manner similar to yoga.

The purpose of burning incense before a spiritual practice is mainly to engage in the mental act of activating the positive energy resulting from refraining from the Ten Negative Actions and cultivating the Ten Positive Actions. This positive energy is visualized as pervading all of space, just as the scent of the incense pervades all of space.

When making an incense offering, the following prayer should be made:

May this act of burning incense serve as the ethical seed for peace,
happiness, and harmony to arise at all existing levels,
from home to the universe.

One should recite the following mantra upon completion of the incense offering:

Om Sarva Tatha Gatha Sa Pari Vara Dupo Pati Tsa Yeh Soha
I send forth this uplifting fragrant incense to the assembly
of Enlightened Beings and Bodhisattvas with their retinue, the
ultimate source of refuge and the path to Enlightenment.

Part Six

ILLUMINATING LIGHT OFFERING

Light. The traditional light offering (Aloka or Dipa) is a butter lamp. The cup (chokong) can be made of gold, silver, copper, brass, or iron. The fuel should be clarified butter, vegetable oil, or beeswax. The light offering may also be in the form of a candle or a small electric or battery-operated light. No fat from the body of an animal should be used. The recommended fuels burn slowly with little smoke. The wick should be made of cotton, never silk, because burning silk smells like burned meat. The flame should be illuminating, calming, gentle, and steady, not flickering. When the light is extinguished, a snuffer should be used rather than blowing with the breath.

The spiritual significance of the light offering is that the flame represents the wisdom realizing emptiness, the wick represents ignorance, and the fuel represents samsara.

When making a light offering, the following prayer should be made:

May this light dispel the darkness of ignorance of all sentient beings and may the wisdom realizing emptiness be quickly developed in the minds of all sentient beings to completely destroy the root cause of samsara, just as the flame destroys the wick and the wax.

One should recite the following mantra upon completion of the light offering:

Om Sarva Tatha Gatha Sa Pari Vara Aloka Pati Tsa Yeh Soha
I send forth this illuminating light to the assembly of Enlightened Beings and Bodhisattvas with their retinue, the ultimate source of refuge and the path to Enlightenment.

Part Seven

FRESH AND HIGH QUALITY FRUIT OFFERING

Fruit Offering. This offering (Naivdya) may be any type of fresh fruit with excellent qualities of shape, color, smell, taste, and texture. Fruit gathered from the wild may be used. High quality biscuits or cookies may be used, but fruit is preferable. The size of the fruit offered can be correlated with the general size of your altar and may vary from a single perfect berry to a large apple. When making a fruit offering, guard against the thought that the fruit is too good for an offering or that it is going to waste. There should be no sense of reluctance or attachment, but only a sense of joy. When the fruit is no longer fresh, it may be disposed of in nature as a food for birds or squirrels, or you may eat it if it is replaced by another fresh offering.

The purpose of a fruit offering is to create merit that dispels the sufferings of poverty, hunger, and malnutrition among all sentient beings in all realms of existence.

When making the offering, you may say:

May this act of offering fruit dispel the sufferings of poverty, hunger, and malnutrition among all sentient beings in all realms of existence.

One should recite the following mantra upon completion of the fruit offering:

Om Sarva Tatha Gatha Sa Pari Vara Naivdya Pati Tsa Yeh Soha
I send forth this fresh fruit (with excellent qualities of smell, taste, color, shape, and nurturing) to the assembly of Enlightened Beings and Bodhisattvas with their retinue, the ultimate source of refuge and the path to Enlightenment.

Part Eight

EAR APPEALING MUSIC OFFERING

Music Offering (Shabta). Using a bell, cymbal, small trumpet, hand drum, or singing bowl may represent the offering of sound. Sound symbolizes the wisdom realizing emptiness – the lack of intrinsic existence of all external and internal phenomena. Simply thinking that all things are empty is insufficient. Through study and learning, you should develop some real understanding that all things lack any substantiality on their own part that would justify the fluctuating feelings of attraction and aversion that we experience when we perceive them with our deluded minds. In one moment, an object may appear to us as attractive and we react with attachment. In the next moment, the same object may appear as unattractive and we react with aversion. Do these feelings truly exist as part of the object? If so, how can the object change momentarily? Who or what determines the qualities of the object? With contemplation and reasoning, we can conclude that the qualities do not reside in the object and that the object lacks intrinsic existence.

While holding this understanding, make a music offering with a wish:

May this act of offering music help to create merit for all sentient beings to overcome ignorance and the mind grasping at things as inherently real.

Music offerings also create merit that is effective in developing a melodious voice that attracts sentient beings to Dharma and to virtuous practices. A music offering helps us to overcome the misperception that the agent, the action, and the object are real. The agent is the doer, the action is what is done, and the object of the action is the recipient of the action. All are empty of intrinsic existence.

One should recite the following mantra upon completion of the music offering:

Om Sarva Tatha Gatha Sa Pari Vara Shabta Pati Tsa Yeh Soha

I send forth this ear soothing music to the assembly of Enlightened Beings and Bodhisattvas with their retinue, the ultimate source of refuge and the path to Enlightenment.

Additional Offerings for Dharma Centers and Temples:

In addition to the above fresh material offerings, one may put money on the altars of Dharma centers or temples as an offering. The money will be used for buying basic daily needs, such as fresh flowers, incense, and candles that monks use every day before doing our daily practice. The money may also be used for repairing and renovating the statues, thangkhas, stupas, and other sacred images, as well as printing practice manual guide booklets and making them available to practitioners in the meditation room or shrine room.

Part Nine

INSTRUCTIONS OF WHAT ONE SHOULD DO AFTER BEAUTIFULLY ARRANGING THE MATERIAL OFFERINGS

When all of the offerings have been arranged and the recitations made, if you have time, sit on a meditation cushion facing the altar. The traditional three prostrations may be done before being seated or after arising. Contemplate the altar as an external secondary aid to generate actual sincere feelings of trust, devotion, and admiration for the spiritual qualities of Enlightened Beings. Cultivate the desire to acquire these qualities for yourself.

With a sense of spiritual comfort in your mind, say the following refuge prayer three times while reflecting on the meaning:

Namo Guru Saranam Gacha Mey
Namo Buddham Saranam Gacha Mey
Namo Dhammam Saranam Gacha Mey
Namo Sangham Saranam Gacha Mey

I take refuge in the Lama.
I take refuge in the Buddha.
I take refuge in the Dharma.
I take refuge in the Sangha.

Taking refuge in the Lama means that you recognize the Lama as the source of the unbroken lineage of teachings that originated with an Enlightened Being. Taking refuge in the Buddha is your recognition of Buddha as the ultimate, flawless spiritual guide. Taking refuge in the Dharma signals your awareness of the Dharma as the peaceful path that leads to the peaceful result of Enlightenment and reaffirms your commitment to follow that path.

Taking refuge in the Sangha means that you recognize those who have already attained the highest levels of spiritual development as examples of courage and determination.

The next step is to generate genuine love (metta) for all sentient beings. Biased and discriminatory thoughts and attitudes should be repressed. Genuine love can only arise when we can see every being as equally dear to our hearts. Heartfelt love spontaneously gives rise to a deep sense of concern and a wish for others to be happy.

Once you have generated love, generating compassion (karuna) is easier and leads to further concern for the well being of others. Understanding of various types of pain and suffering that sentient beings experience gives rise to a spontaneous feeling of the unbearableness of their suffering and a wish and a willingness to dispel that suffering if help is within your means and capabilities. This compassion is different from merely feeling sympathy and relating to other's suffering.

Until we become Bodhisattvas, we will lack the clairvoyance to fully see the real needs of others and we will lack the perfected skillful means to relieve their suffering.

However, within our means and capabilities, we should help others as much as we can.

While your mind and heart are saturated with feelings of love and compassion, recite the Invitation Prayer, asking all Enlightened Beings to witness and preside over your sincere efforts in making offerings:

Ma Lus Sen Chen Kun Gyi Gon Gyur Chig
The ultimate guide of all sentient beings without exception,

Du Dhe Pung Chey Mee Sey Zom Zey Lha
One who has overcome the army force of Mara,

Ngo Nam Ma Lus Yang Dak Kyen Gyur Pey
And one who knows all phenomena directly with the omniscient mind that leaves nothing,

Com Den Kor Che Ney Dir Sheg Su Sol.
May I request all the Buddhas to be present here instantly with their retinue.

Lha Dang Mee Yi Cho Pay Zey
The clean and pure offerings, from heavenly and human realms,

Ngo Su Sham Dang Yee Kyi Trul
Both real and imagined,

Kun Zang Cho Trin Lana Mey
The clouds of offerings with excellent qualities of shape, smell, taste, color, and texture,

Nam Kay Kyon Kun Kyab Gyur Chik!
May these offerings become as vast as the sky and reach beyond our ordinary imagination!

Recitation of the following Mantra of Interdependent Arising helps to increase and multiply material offerings in number and quality, and purifies the offering substances from the contamination of your delusions, such as attachment, ego, impure mundane intentions, and the false notion of inherent existence:

Namo Ratna Trayaya! Namo Bhagavate! Bhen Zah Sara Trama Dahney!
Tatha Gataya! Arya Hatey Samya Buddha Ya! Taya Tha!
Om Ben Zey Ben Zey! Maha Ben Zey! Maha Tey Zah Ben Zey!
Maha Bhi Ya Ben Zey! Maha Bho Dhi Teh Tsa Ben Zey!
Maha Bodhi Mendro! Pak Sam Tra Ma Na Ben Zey!
Sava Kama Ava Ratna Bhi Sho Dana Ben Zey So Ha!

Om Ah Hung (Recite three times.)

Om – Seed syllable that purifies impurities of color, odor, taste, nurturing, and the life sustaining force of the offering substances.

Ah – Seed syllable that transforms the offering substances into the ambrosia and nectar of the wisdom realizing emptiness.

Hung – Seed syllable that multiplies the offering substances boundlessly and reaches beyond the limitations of your dualistic mind.

Part Ten

FINAL DEDICATION PRAYERS FOR CLOSING YOUR OFFERING PRACTICE WITH THE AWARENESS OF EMPTINESS IN ALL PHENOMENA

Next come the Dedication Prayers, the sincere act of dedicating your merit and virtuous deeds to a higher purpose for the happiness of others and to dispel the miseries of the world. You may choose any prayer or prayers that reflect the dedication you wish to make.

May there be no illness, dispute or war
At all existing levels, from home to the universe.
May everyone experience joy, peace, and spiritual splendors.
May the glory and richness of goodness ever increase!

May all sentient beings experience joy and happiness,
And may all unfortunate births be ceased.
Wherever Bodhisattvas abide and make their unselfish prayers,
May their prayers come true and bear results.

In all the directions, whoever is mentally and physically
In pain from whatever ailments,
May my merit be the cause for them
To experience an ocean of joy and bliss.

Bodhicitta is precious,
May those who have not engendered it, engender it;
May those who have engendered it, not lose it.
May it always grow and increase.

May I never dwell on the desire to fulfill my own interests.
May I solely strive for the benefit of others.
May all necessary ways to benefit others, such as wisdom eyes,
Clairvoyance, skillful ways to speak, patience, and so forth,
May I possess all of these benefiting qualities quickly.

To close your offering practice, bring your mind to a deep awareness of emptiness. Reflect on the emptiness of all things and phenomena without having a sense of any agent, action, and object of action as being inherently existent. The perfected wisdom realizing emptiness is the ultimate antidote to the grasping, clinging, and ignorance that keeps all sentient beings mired in the suffering of conventional existence.

CONCLUSION OF ALTAR OFFERINGS

The practice of offering material objects to the Enlightened Beings and Bodhisattvas with a clean motivation and respectful attitude is one of the most important factors for spiritual development. It is one of the most effective means for the accumulation of merit. Merit is a positive energy or force that is naturally conducive to smooth spiritual growth with few obstructions and hindrances.

Lord Buddha often advised his followers about the importance of merit-making practices and the major role merit plays in spiritual practice and the process of gaining spiritual realization. Buddha said in the Sutra:

Merit gives rise to happiness and fortune; it eliminates the causes of pain and failure in all worldly and spiritual achievements. The wishes and aspirations of the person who is rich in merit will easily be fulfilled without struggle.

All of our fortune and good things occur as a direct result of meritorious karma and all misfortune and tragedy occur as a result of de-meritorious karma. The external circumstances are just a temporary contributing condition for meritorious and de-meritorious karma to bring their results. The external circumstances are not the primary cause for our fortune or misfortune, happiness or pain, success or failure. No good or positive things can occur when there is a lack of merit, no matter how smart, intelligent, or hard working you are. You will not succeed in anything. So, everything is surely not within your means and effort. There is a real need to have merit behind your means and effort in order to succeed in worldly and spiritual achievements.

Merit-making practices are extremely important and necessary for a smooth and consistent spiritual growth without struggle and disheartening obstacles. The above listed material offerings are an extremely effective and powerful way to accumulate merit, even if it is only a small offering. If you have only made material offerings for a short period of time, it is still beneficial. The practice of offering material objects to the Enlightened Beings and Bodhisattvas is pretty easy to do no matter how busy you are in your daily life.

Creating merit through offering material objects to Enlightened Beings is superior to other ways of fulfilling your wishes and aspirations – whatever they may be. Integrating the practice of offering material objects with your major practices of love, compassion, generosity, ethics, patience, forgiveness, stabilizing meditation, and penetrative insight meditation into the ultimate truth of emptiness of all things, events, and phenomena completes the path to Enlightenment.

Being rich in material wealth is only useful in this life. Hoarding what you have does not help you in the next life because when you die, you must leave all your material wealth behind. You cannot reclaim it in the next life. On the other hand, being rich in merit, spiritual knowledge, and wisdom is beneficial both in the present life as well as in your future life. You can reclaim merit, spiritual knowledge, and wisdom as yours in the next life. And not only can you reclaim these, but also, you will be reborn into a wealthy home, you will be intelligent, successful, knowledgeable and wise, courageous and generous, compassionate, healthy, and naturally predisposed to meritorious deeds and actions. And if you continue to create merit, you will go through an uninterrupted spiritual evolution towards Enlightenment, from fortunate life to fortunate life, as a result of your wealth of merit.

If you do not practice the offering of material objects to Enlightened Beings and Bodhisattvas, thinking that you are above this simple practice, you are making a grave and unfortunate error. This attitude itself becomes a serious obstacle to your other practices and delays the attainment of Enlightenment. It will make you encounter many external and internal hindrances and disheartening struggles in your training process on the paths and grounds. Be serious in your merit-making practices and you will surely accumulate immeasurable amounts of merit as vast as the ocean and as plentiful as the grains of sand in the ocean.

SECTION TWO

PRACTICAL AND SPIRITUAL ADVICE:
BUDDHIST PRACTICES FOR DAILY LIFE USING
YOUR PERSONAL ALTAR

The purpose of this guide is to assist Buddhists with how to live in the day-to-day world and incorporate Buddhist practices into our busy lives. We often feel that we are so busy that we put off thinking about our Buddhist selves, and instead focus on our daily routines and obligations. But if we learn to take time, especially at the beginning and end of the day for Buddhist practices, we can start to see benefits that can make us lead happier and better lives.

A) Upon Awakening: How to Start the Day

When we wake up, before getting out of bed, our first thoughts should be to remind ourselves that we are Buddhists. It is important to acknowledge this in a humble and genuine way, with no arrogance. These thoughts should come deeply from your heart.

Turn your mind to focus on the Buddha, the Dharma, and the Sangha as your primary objects of refuge. Refresh your awareness of who the Buddha was and why you follow him.

Ask yourself why you study and practice the Dharma. Think about whom the Sangha is and why you respect and hold them in deep regard.

After you have reflected on these, briefly take refuge and recite the following mantra three times while contemplating its meaning:

Namo Guru Saranam Gacha Mey
Namo Buddham Saranam Gacha Mey
Namo Dhammam Saranam Gacha Mey
Namo Sangham Saranam Gacha Mey

I take refuge in the Lama
I take refuge in the Buddha
I take refuge in the Dharma
I take refuge in the Sangha

Upon reciting the refuge formula, refresh your trust, respect, devotion, and determination to stay with the Buddha's teachings. (In lieu of doing this practice before getting out of bed, one may choose to do this practice before beginning your daily routine.)

B) How to Live During the Day

Four Daily Offerings:

If you follow the teachings of Tibetan Buddhism, you may then perform the following four daily offerings. These offerings may be at your home altar or on a small table. The very purpose of making these offerings is either to create merit, or to purify negative karmic obstructions. The individual's intentions will determine the purpose of the offerings.

1) Water offerings. There is no fixed number of bowls, but seven bowls is the traditional number used in the Tibetan custom.

The water offerings are divided into the following types:

a) Fresh and clear water offering for drinking

b) Scented water offering for washing feet or bathing

You may divide the types of water offerings among the seven bowls, with the fresh and clear water offering given first priority. If available, you may put a drop of rose water or saffron into the scented water offering bowls. If not available, all seven bowls may be filled with fresh, clear water.

The fresh and clear water offering generates awareness of the means to free all sentient beings from the sufferings of thirst. It aims to benefit them with soothing and refreshing drinking water, which is harmless to the throat and stomach and aids digestion.

One should recite the following mantra upon completion of the clear water offering:

Om Sarva Tatha Gatha Sa Pari Vara Argam Pati Tsa Yeh Soha

I send forth this clean and fresh water to the assembly of Enlightened Beings and Bodhisattvas with their retinue, the ultimate source of refuge and the path to Enlightenment.

The scented water offering for bathing or washing feet helps enhance the function of the nervous system by promoting optimal circulation of blood and energy, and to aid our general physical health. The purpose of washing one's feet before an image of the Buddha is to create merit for all sentient beings to develop pure ethical conduct that will enhance their healthy spiritual development.

Upon completion of the scented water offering, recite the following mantra:

Om Sarva Tatha Gatha Sa Pari Vara Gandha Pati Tsa
Yeh Soha

*I send forth this scented water to the assembly of Enlightened Beings
and Bodhisattvas with their retinue, the ultimate source of refuge
and the path to Enlightenment.*

2) Candlelight offering. The type of candle to use is made
of beeswax, vegetable oil, or clarified butter. Candles made
from animal fat are not be used. The wick should be made
of cotton, never silk, as burning silk smells like burned
meat. The flame should be illuminating, calming, gentle,
steady, and not flickering.

The spiritual significance of the candle offering is that the
flame represents wisdom realizing emptiness, the wick
represents ignorance, and the wax represents samsara.

The following prayer should be spoken while making the
light offering:

*May this light dispel the darkness of ignorance of all sentient beings
and may the wisdom realizing emptiness be quickly developed in the
minds of all sentient beings to completely destroy the root cause of
samsara just as the flame destroys the wick and the wax.*

3) Incense offering. One should burn incense with the
awareness of the spiritual significance of the fragrance of
the incense. The safest and best incense to use is Tibetan
hand-made incense with all natural ingredients. The use of

other types of incense may contain chemicals, other artificial ingredients, and traces of animal blood.

The main purpose of burning incense is to engage in the mental act of activating positive energy resulting from the ten negative actions and cultivating the ten positive actions. The positive energy is visualized as pervading all of space, just as the scent of the incense pervades all of space.

When making an incense offering, the following prayer should be made:

May this act of burning incense serve as the ethical seed for peace, happiness, and harmony to arise at all existing levels, from home to the universe.

The following mantra should be recited upon completing the incense offering:

Om Sarva Tatha Gatha Sa Pari Vara Dupo Pati Tsa Yeh Soha I send forth this uplifting fragrant incense to the assembly of Enlightened Beings and Bodhisattvas with their retinue, the ultimate source of refuge and the path to Enlightenment.

4) Music offering. The offering of sound may be represented by a bell, cymbal, small trumpet, hand drum, or singing bowl. Sound symbolizes the wisdom realizing emptiness – the lack of intrinsic existence of all external and internal phenomena. Simply thinking that all things are empty is insufficient.

Through study and learning, you should develop some real understanding that all things lack any substantiality on their own part that would justify feelings of attraction and aversion.

With this understanding, make the music offering with this wish:

May this act of offering music help to create merit for all sentient beings to overcome ignorance and the mind grasping at things as inherently real.

Music offerings help us to overcome the misperception that the agent, the action, and the object are real.

The agent is the doer, the action is what is done, and the object of the action is the recipient of the action. All are empty of intrinsic existence.

The following mantra is to be recited after completing the music offering:

Om Sarva Tatha Gatha Sa Pari Vara Shabta Pati Tsa Yeh Soha
I send forth this ear-soothing music to the assembly of Enlightened Beings and Bodhisattvas with their retinue,
the ultimate source of refuge and the path to Enlightenment.

Making Prostrations:

Making prostrations is an important part of daily practice. Prostrations show devotion, humility, and respect.

One should perform a minimum of three or more prostrations daily.

To do short prostrations, the following procedures should be followed:

- Stand with your feet straight ahead and slightly apart.

- Your body posture should be erect.

- Stand in front of your altar, or an image of Buddha, or a holy text while keeping your mind focused on the image.

- Be mindful of being in the present moment.

- Your hands should be cupped together with the tips of your fingers touching the fingers of your opposite hand. Your thumbs are tucked inside the cupped hands touching the inside of your ring fingers.

- With cupped hands, touch the crown of your head, then your throat, and then your heart.

- During the prostrations, your hands should first make contact with the floor, then your knees, and finally your forehead.

- Return to the standing position and repeat two or more times.

While carrying out the prostrations, say the following mantra:

Om Namo Manjushri Ye
Namo Sushri Ye
Namo Utamma Shriye Soha

For more information on prostrations, please refer to pages 22-26 from *Holistic Health: A Tibetan Monk's View,* by Geshe Dakpa Topgyal.

Silent Meditation:

After completing the prostrations, sit in silent meditation for ten to fifteen minutes to refresh your mind and motivate yourself to live each day in a meaningful and mindful way. One should try as much as one can to spend each day doing good and staying away from harmful actions and deeds. Refresh mindful skills to control one's thoughts and emotions.

Devote oneself to live with this mind skill for the remainder of the day.

Your Daily Routine:

It is then time to begin your daily conventional routine. However, this does not mean forgetting about how to spend the day living as a Buddhist. One has a natural feeling of "I am a human". But, one can also have a natural feeling of "I am a Buddhist".

This involves being discerning about what is right and what is wrong, what is useful and what is not useful, and what is appropriate and what is inappropriate. To do so, one needs to be more watchful about making judgments and being less judgmental of others. One needs to be more introspective, with a willingness to see one's errors and correct oneself.

One needs to be less emotional and be more aware of how feelings affect our lives. One needs to have less bias and truly analyze the different aspects of situations. In addition, one needs to learn to limit talking by discussing what is useful instead of what is not useful and unnecessary. It is often wise to remain in noble silence.

For the remainder of the day, the following suggestions may be helpful in leading a good, wholesome, and happy life"

- Do not bring work problems home, nor take family problems to work.

- It is better not to make decisions while under the influence of emotions, as all emotions can cloud our decisions.
- Train the mind to let thoughts rest on the Dharma with whatever we are doing.
- Do not leave compassion at home, nor take aggression into the world.

C) In the Evening: How to End the Day

If you have some free time in the evening, you may conclude the day with the following practices.

Before retiring to bed, go before your altar or table to light a candle and burn a stick of incense to help gain awareness. With this awareness, make three prostrations. Then, while sitting on your cushion or in a chair, do a brief mental review of the day's events – what you did, said, and thought. Analyze with complete candor what actions were right or wrong, and whether you have any regrets of those actions. Make a resolve not to repeat the negative actions by means of being mindful of your actions as much as you can. Imagine that all Enlightened Beings are bearing witness to your resolve.

With your mind in a calm and peaceful state, take time for ten to fifteen minutes of silent meditation. The time spent to do this meditation will help lead to an uninterrupted, restful sleep. The next morning, you will awaken with a body and mind that is fresh, rejuvenated, and energetic.

Another important aspect to be analyzed every evening is to briefly contemplate one's life. This present life is precious and meaningful, and has numerous opportunities for moral and spiritual growth. We need to remember that life is extremely fragile – like a dewdrop, a snowflake, a bolt of lightning, a rainbow, a mirage, and a water bubble. Our life has no fixed time to live, nor can our lifespan be extended. It rapidly diminishes day by day.

Life dwells in the causes and conditions for death, as there are many more causes and conditions for death than for life to continue living. Because of these reasons, death is sure and certain. Death cannot be prevented, just like a waterfall cannot be reversed.

However, since death is a natural part of life, it is not a personal tragedy, nor an ultimate failure of our life. One may ask: What matters most to my life... to live ethically, to give love and care to others, and to die in peace? Make sure to try to cultivate these three wishes.

We are fortunate to have lived to the present day. However, it is undetermined to know if we have another day to live, and whether we will wake up the next morning.

It is highly possible not to awaken, as life has more conditions to die than to live. One may die today or tomorrow, but there is more probability than we may die today rather than tomorrow.

Most of us die sooner than we think we will – an "unexpected" death. But there is no such thing as an unexpected death. Death is always expected. With this awareness of the fragility of life, we can go to bed more humbly with hope to have another day to live. If not, then we should pray to die peacefully in the eyewitness of the Lord Buddha.

APPENDIX

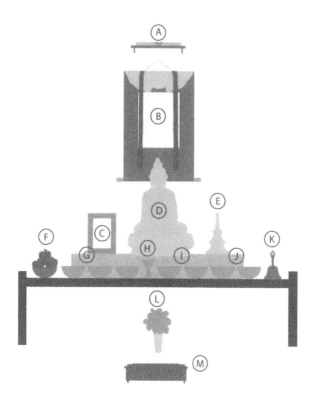

SAMPLE ATLAR Set Up and Offerings

A) Heart Sutra

B) Thangkha

C) Maitreya image

D) Buddha image

E) Stupa

F) Fresh fruit

G) Fresh water for drinking

H) Illuminating light

I) Scented water for bathing

J) Scented water for washing feet

K) Ear-appealing music

L) Fresh flowers

M) Natural incense

ABOUT THE AUTHOR

GESHE DAKPA TOPGYAL

Geshe-la obviously has all the Buddhist knowledge and personal experience, and he reflects that with his calmness but also with an incredible sense of humor.
He uses his amazing vocabulary to express complex concepts according to everyone's individual mental activity.
~Charleston Magazine

Geshe Dakpa Topgyal, a Tibetan Buddhist monk, was born in the Western region of Tibet, and fled to India at the age of six with his family, due to the Chinese invasion of Tibet. He entered Drepung Loseling Monastery at the age of ten and received the Geshe degree (Doctorate of

Religion and Philosophy) twenty-two years later in 1992. Before coming to the United States, he taught in Europe for several years. He has been resident monk of the Charleston Tibetan Society in Charleston, South Carolina since 1996. Geshe La has written several books on Buddhism.